UNDERSTANDING MASS SHOOTINGS

MICHAEL R. WEISSER

Copyright 2022.

ISBN: 9798352557358

CONTENTS

INTRODUCTION.

INTRODUCTION.

It's light outside. The house is dark inside. The kid is getting dressed, quietly, not making a sound. He needs to lace his shoes tight so that he can walk without making any noise. He can hear his mother breathing, sleeping in her bed, face down. Always face down.

Now quietly, without a sound, he goes down the hall to the rec room where the gun safe is against the wall opposite the TV. He knows the combination by heart. He has opened the safe countless times. He has shot all the guns that are in the safe.

The safe door swings open. The kid reaches in and wraps his hand around the barrel of the Marlin rifle, model XP, the first real gun he ever shot. His father took him to the range when he was fourteen years old – now he's twenty – and let him shoot this gun.

"It's *your* gun," the father said to him that day. "Here's how you hold it."

Now he's holding the gun the same way he held it on the range. Barrel pointing away and towards the ground, hand around the stock but finger off the trigger.

"You put your finger on the trigger when you're ready to shoot the gun," said his father, "and that's only when you're pointing the gun at the target you want to shoot."

The kid is now standing, four feet away from the target he wants to shoot. Lifts the gun to his shoulder, plants his feet, aims, pulls the trigger. The bullet, a 16-grain, 22LR-caliber piece of lead mixed with a bit of ammonium nitrate hits the exact spot the kid wanted to hit – the base of his mother's skull.

Her body jerks slightly as the bullet enters her brain. She makes no sound. She is dead and the kid knows she is dead.

He turns away and starts walking back down the hall. Before he gets back to the gun safe, he grasps the rifle bolt in his right hand, flips up and then pulls back to eject the empty shell. Never leave a spent shell in the breech of a gun, his father taught him. The powder will corrode the barrel; and the gun won't be accurate or worse, could jam.

The kid places the Marlin rifle back in the safe and lifts out another gun. This one is a Bushmaster Model XPS, and there are three fully loaded, 30-shot magazines for this gun on a shelf in the safe where there is also a loaded handgun, a 9mm Sig pistol Model 3022R.

The kid also takes the pistol out of the safe, closes the door. Now the gun safe is locked which is how it should always be. He was taught that too.

Finishes getting dressed. A jacket over the shirt with side pockets for the pistol and the extra mags. A hoodie over his head.

It takes the kid twelve minutes to drive from his house to the elementary school. When he was a student at the school, he usually was picked up by a school bus. Now he's twenty years old and he left the school eight years ago. How many times has he driven from his house to the school in the last month? Twenty times? Thirty times? More? He didn't count.

Now he is parking in front of the school. Sits in the car and looks around. All the students are inside the building. The kid made sure that he would only arrive at the school when everyone was inside.

Here's the tricky part. He has to walk up the twenty paces from his car to the school's entrance door. He knows it's twenty paces because he has counted the steps again and again while he was making his plan.

But this is the first time he is making the approach to the school's front entrance with an assault rifle in his hands. Not to be seen until he gets inside the school because otherwise the whole plan which he has worked on for months might not happen the way it's supposed to happen.

The kid has 90 rounds of military-grade ammunition in his three magazines. Two of the magazines are taped together in a way which lets him flip an empty mag over and reload the gun with a full mag in two seconds or less. He has practiced releasing the empty mag, flipping the full mag over and inserting it into the gun hundreds of times.

The kid walks up to the school entrance. The door is locked but he has taken this into account while making his plans. Around the door are small panes of glass which are resistant to someone pushing against them. The glass is thick and reinforced, but shatters instantly when the kid shoots two rounds from his rifle through one of the panes, which allows him to reach through, grab the inside door handle, twist, pull and the door swings open wide.

The noise of the gunshots draws the school's principal, Dawn Hochsprung, out into the hall. During her two-year tenure, the school had instituted a new security system that relied on everyone who wanted access to the building being issued a permanent or temporary ID. But the office which controls school security isn't yet open, which is why the front entrance was locked. The principal, in a meeting with her guidance staff, knows that something is wrong when she hears the gunshots, which is why she is the first person to see the kid as he started walking down the hall.

She sees him for maybe ten seconds, which is how long it takes the kid to bring the rifle up to eye-level and squeeze off several rounds which hit Dawn Hochsprung and now there are two dead.

Kid walks down the hall, enters the first classroom to the right. Shoots off 40 – 50 rounds, kills 14 first grade kids, injures 7 more including the teacher.

Exits the classroom, takes a few steps, and goes into the next room where he shoots and kills another 11 children, wounds 9 more.

Altogether he has fired some 90 rounds in less than 3 minutes. Tries to enter a third room but the door is locked. The teacher in that room had enough time to save herself and the children in her room.

Kid pushes the door once or twice. It stays closed. Sirens can be heard outside the school.

Kid lays down the rifle, pulls the pistol out of his jacket pocket and shoots himself in the head.

It takes about the same amount of time to read the above description of what happened as it took Adam Lanza to shoot, kill and wound 26 children and adults at the Sandy Hook Elementary School in Newtown, CT on December 12, 2012.

This was hardly the first mass shooting, nor was it the first time that young boys, just out of their teens, walked into a school and committed multiple murders of teachers and children. In fact, it was the killing of 14 students at the high school in Columbine, CO in 1999, which began to create a public consciousness about this particular type of violent behavior in the United States.

Even though some of the more fervent pro-gun advocates have tried to make the argument that spraying a large mass of human beings with military-grade ammunition which creates injuries in double-digit populations occurs in every country, not just in the United States, it was not until the Sandy Hook massacre that we began to see shootings that resulted in ten, twenty, thirty or even more fatal and non-fatal injuries as being uniquely American events

But where such events occur on a frequent basis in other countries we are talking about organized acts of terror or civil warfare between conflicting groups. We are not talking about some isolated, teen-age kid who parks himself in front of his computer for several months, figures out where and when would be the optimum place and time to commit an act of mass carnage, and then busies himself putting together the weapon, the ammunition and the plan that will enable him to carry out this event.

A year following the massacre at Sandy Hook, the FBI released an official report on mass shootings which was prompted by a new law, the *Investigative Assistance for Violent Crimes Act of 2012,* which gave the Department of Justice authority to assist in the investigation of "violent acts and shootings occurring in a place of public use" and "mass killings and attempted mass killings" in any public space.

The FBI has continued to track and monitor mass shootings, with their most recent report covering these events in 2020. The research in these reports has resulted in the word 'mass' being replaced by the word 'active,' because some of these shootings have involved a perpetrator moving from one physical site to another during the continuous commission of these violent crimes, and the FBI's intention is to focus on what might be done or should be done by law enforcement during the commission of such crimes.

From 2000 through 2013, the FBI identified 160 mass shooting events which met their criteria for inclusion, for an average of 11.4 events each year. In 2016 there were 20 such shootings, a number which doubled to 40 mass shootings in 2020, an astonishing increase in just four years.

In 2018 and 2019, the number of victims identified by the FBI as being shot and killed by 'active shooters' was 141 individuals out of 78,000 Americans who died from intentional gun shootings over those two years. Even if we were to estimate the victim numbers for the type of mass shootings which the FBI excludes from their research, the total number of such fatalities would probably be no more than 400.

For the five years from 2016 through 2020, which includes the 56 killed at the rock concert in Las Vegas in 2017, the FBI count gets us up to slightly over 450. Doubling that number to take into account the mass shootings not included in the FBI report, and we are still less than one-half of one percent of the number of shooting victims killed during those five years.

However, in 2022, something else has been added to the mass shooting mix. On May 17th, 2022, an 18-year-old drove 200 miles from his home to Buffalo, NY, entered a supermarket, shot 10 people fatally and wounded 3 more. On May 24th, another eighteen-year-old shot his grandmother, then drove to an elementary school in Uvalde, TX, entered the building and proceeded to kill and wound 37 children and staff. On July 4th, a 21-year-old killed 7 and wounded more than 30 others who were marching in a July 4th parade in the Chicago suburb of Highland Park, IL.

In less than eight weeks, three mass shootings occurred which killed and injured more than 80 persons, traumatized three communities, and forced a reluctant federal government to enact the first and decidedly mild gun restriction law in more than twenty-five years. This number of fatal and non-fatal injuries in such a brief period of time does not appear in any other advanced country where residents enjoy a level of public safety and security that we assume exists throughout the developed world. It only happens in the United States. Why?

The FBI studies on active shooting situations go into precise and detailed information about the kinds of individuals who commit these mass-killing events. We know their age, gender, employment, and education. We know whether they dressed in protective clothing for the attack, whether they committed suicide after the attack, whether they were apprehended by police or were prevented from committing more mayhem because a civilian onlooker intervened.

What we do not know about a single perpetrator is what kind of weapon or weapons were used to commit these mass assaults. What this book will explain is the causal connection between the types of weapons which are used by shooters who commit mass carnage in public spaces, and how and why the gun industry promotes this behavior by consciously developing and marketing products which will appeal to individuals who are thinking about killing as many people as possible occupying a public space. And such products are increasingly made available to prospective purchasers through finance plans designed for younger people who normally do not have the financial resources to purchase these kinds of guns.

The United States is the only advanced country (or unadvanced country, for that matter) which allows its residents to acquire certain types of weapons designed to be used specifically for these kinds of massive-killing events.

Before we go further into the discussion about mass shooting events, however, we need to clarify one other aspect issue related to the nomenclature used to discuss this issue in both the pro=gun and gun-control communities, as well as in the popular media and daily press.

When the phrase 'mass shooting' appears in those venues, however, it is usually being applied to shootings in which 4 individuals in the same location are killed or are wounded and killed.

Those shootings are not the subject of this book. First, the adoption of four victims, dead or alive, as qualifying a shooting as a 'mass' shooting, is entirely arbitrary, and came about at a meeting of researchers in which a majority of the attendees believed that a numeric of this amount was the proper way to define the word 'mass.' Why didn't this group decide that a proper numeric definition should have been three, or five? Nobody remembers and nobody knows.

The mass shootings which are the subject of this book are not only distinctive in terms of the number of victims, with double digits being the minimum number of victims for being considered herein, but these also events had long-lasting and overwhelmingly drastic consequences on the entire community in which the shootings occurred. Many community residents beyond the immediate circle of the families and friends of the victims were traumatized in serious and continuous ways. Buildings where mass shootings occurred were torn down permanently or closed down for months at a time.

But to understand the phenomena of mass shootings which form the basis of this book, there is a much more important distinction which needs to be made, a distinction based on the relationship between perpetrator and victim or victims in the two different categories of gun assaults.

In the case of the average homicide event, even events which yield multiple victims, the two parties are almost always known to one another before the killing or attempted killing takes place. They may be members of the same family, they may live next door to one another, they may be engaged in some common endeavor, financial or otherwise. Usually for one reason or another, the two parties have been engaged in some kind of ongoing dispute which eventually gets out of hand, leading to a verbal or physical threat, at which point one of the disputants pulls out a gun.

Mass shootings discussed in this text, however, are rarely motivated by the shooter wanting to inflict a serious injury on a particular individual and for reasons of happenstance or accident other individuals get in the way. Many mass shootings take place in public spaces which are known by the shooter, such as a school which he attended as a student or a mall or theater where he spent time watching a movie or just moving around.

The mass shooter will often select a physical location which he knows well enough to give him the information he needs to plan the attack as well as a possible escape. But these choices reflect the pre-event planning which often goes into how a mass shooter decides where he wants to stage his assault and does not necessarily demonstrate that he has any personal connection to the people who he will attempt to shoot.

It should also be mentioned that mass shootings do not happen because someone just wanders around a public space with a gun and then spontaneously or unthinkingly pulls out his weapon and begins to blast away. Over the years, there has been an attempt by pro-gun advocates to promote guns by stressing their use for armed, self-defense, the idea being that a gun's lethality makes the weapon a perfect, self-protective device.

For this reason, nearly all 50 states now allow legal gun owners to carry a weapon on their person without prior licensing for concealed carry of the gun, a procedure recently validated by the Supreme Court as falling under 2nd-Amendment 'rights.' However, there is no connection, arguments to the contrary made by some gun-control advocates, that such procedures encourage mass shooting behavior or mass killing events.

It is a mistake to assume that a mass shooting is no different from a typical street-corner gun assault except that more victims end up in the ER or the morgue. This book will tell a story about mass shootings from the perspective of the types of weapons which show up in such behavior because the individual who wants to kill a lot of people knows that there are certain types or models of guns which make it easier and more efficient to think and plan murders in multiple terms. These weapons are only available for purchase by consumers living in the United States and are weapons whose availability has been promoted for the last several decades.

Thus, we need to move to the substantive portion of this narrative by looking at those guns.

CHAPTER 1. THE GUNS USED IN MASS SHOOTINGS.

From the mid-nineteenth century when handguns were first invented, until the 1970's, the basic material which was used to create a handgun was carbon (i.e., treated) steel. It is treated by mixing steel with an alloy, carbon, which creates a material which is less resistant to rust but becomes harder and stronger when heated prior to being shaped and cut.

In 1836, Samuel Colt was given a patent for a revolver, so named because it reloaded the ammunition by rotating a cylinder through the action of the trigger connected to this cylinder and the hammer. This handgun was manufactured using carbon steel. In 1852, another gunsmith trained at the government arsenal in Springfield, Daniel Wesson, designed and produced his first handgun, which was built around a rotating cylinder which held multiple shells.

Here is a modern version of a revolver which has hardly changed since these guns were first manufactured by Smith & Wesson and Colt:

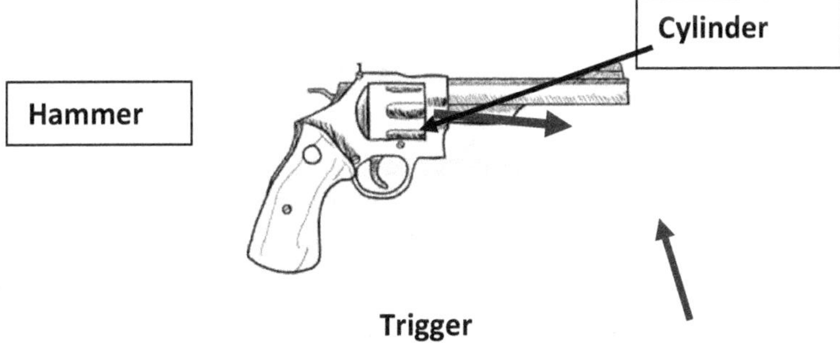

By the end of the nineteenth century, gun makers began to produce the other basic handgun design, known as the semi-automatic pistol, which reloaded itself after each shot was fired, not by the action of the trigger, but by the pressures of the gases that were released by the ignition of the gunpowder behind the bullet.

These pressures both propelled the bullet forward through the barrel, but also pushed the gun's slide backwards, both ejecting the empty shell and pushing a new, unfired round into the barrel of the gun. The most successful semi-automatic design was developed by John Browning in 1903, which eventually became the 45-caliber sidearm adopted by the U.S. Military in   1911:

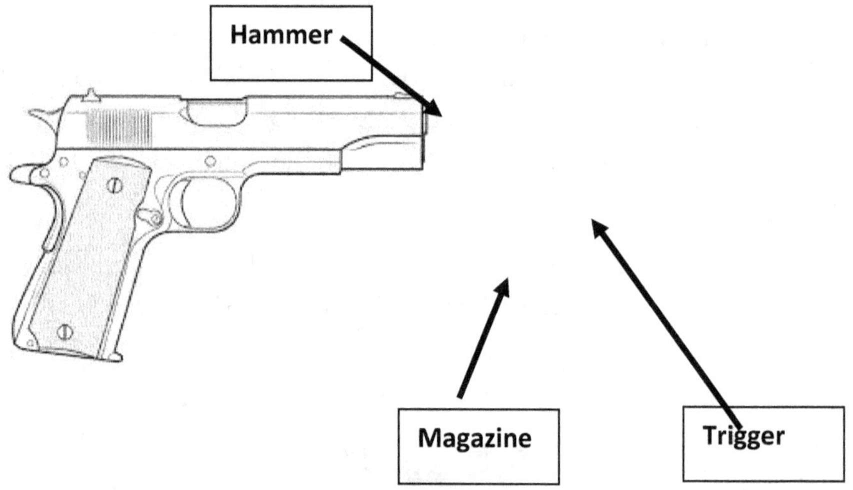

The advantage of the pistol over the revolver was that the magazine could hold more than 6 rounds (the 1911 magazine held 8 rounds) and the gun could be reloaded easily and quickly by pulling the empty magazine out of the handle and replacing it with a fresh, loaded magazine. Reloading the revolver, on the other hand, required a more complicated reloading procedure with each fresh round being individually inserted into the cylinder of the gun.

Even though revolvers continued to represent the more commonly owned handgun in the United States, as opposed to Europe where semi-automatic pistols were the more popular product choice, this would change in the 1970's for reasons having to do with both military and commercial influences on the American handgun market.

To begin, the Colt 1911 pistol, which had probably been the single most copied handgun design of all time, was withdrawn from the American military arsenal in the early 1970's and was replaced by a hi-capacity, double-action, semi-automatic pistol chambered for 9mm ammunition, which was the standard, military round used by all the other NATO troops.

The gun which became the American military handgun was designed by the Italian arms maker Beretta but had to be manufactured within the United States. Beretta refurbished and expanded a small gun factory in Accokeek, MD, across the Potomac River from Mount Vernon, which is now the headquarters and manufacturing facility of Beretta, USA.

Once Beretta became the 'official' U.S. sidearm, the company began promoting this handgun and others both to law enforcement agencies as well as to commercial distributors who then shipped Beretta guns to retail dealers throughout the United States. Almost immediately, other European handgun makers, most notably Glock and Sig-Sauer, also began to move their products into the American market, and by the mid-1980's, semi-automatic pistols which held 14 or more rounds became the handguns of choice for American gun consumers,

The second factor which began to reshape the American gun market with the gradual disappearance of the revolver and its replacement by high-capacity, semi-automatic pistols was a change in state-level gun regulations with the appearance and spread of concealed-carry (CCW) licensing throughout the United States. In 1988, there were only 4 states where residents could carry a concealed gun on their person outside their home without first receiving a specific CCW license requiring them to prove specific need.

By the mid-1990's, a majority of states granted CCW licenses to residents who could pass the same background check required by the 1994 Brady law to purchase a gun. As of 2022, more than 20 states no longer required any kind of specific CCW licensing at all, and in June 2022 the Supreme Court ruled that any kind of CCW licensing which required an applicant to prove specific business or personal need to carry a concealed weapon outside the home was a violation of 2nd-Amendment 'rights.'

The gun industry responded to this fundamental change in gun culture by shifting its products and its marketing narratives away from hunting and sport shooting to products whose primary use would be armed, self-defense. The 1975 Smith & Wesson catalog listed two centerfire, semi-automatic pistols, the Model 37 and the Model 59, the latter a high-capacity version of the Model 39 which the company had submitted to the military to be selected as the gun that would replace the Coly 1911. The Model 59 failed the Army's field-testing procedure which ultimately awarded the contract to Beretta not once, but twice.

The current Smith and Wesson product listings now have more than 30 different semi-automatic, centerfire pistols, most of which are advertised as being designed specifically for concealed carry and armed, self-defense. These guns include models that are designed for female shooters with lightweight slides which can be easily used by individuals with smaller hands. There are also pistols that are small enough to be comfortably carried in jackets or pocketbooks.

The Glock catalog includes a specific 'personal defense' section which contains more than 50 different guns. The most popular gun is the subcompact Model 26, a 9mm pistol which holds 10 rounds and is just six inches long, which makes it slightly longer than my droid. Unloaded, it weighs only slightly more than one pound and if the consumer has the slightest doubt for how this gun was designed, Glock advertises the Model 26 as a 'pocket carry' gun.

When gun makers like Colt and Smith and Wesson first started making and marketing 'pocket carry' guns, they were very small, often less than 4 inches in length and were chambered for calibers like 25acp, which is lethal but only if it hits someone right between the eyes. Here's a picture of the 25-caliber pocket gun designed by John Browning in 1908:

Note the size of the gun relative to the size of the man's hand. Now note the size of a modern pocket gun:

The guns are roughly the same size. However, the Glock shoots a 9mm round which has been the standard, law-enforcement and military ammunition carried by officers and troopers throughout the world since it was developed in the decade before World War I.

How did manufacturing materials and technologies change to allow gun makers to develop small, pocket-sized guns whose pressures when they were fired were strong enough to shoot ammunition that was five times more powerful than the ammunition first used in concealable guns?

Gun makers first started using alloyed rather than full-carbon steel in the 1930's, but then switched from alloys to polymer in the 1970's after Gaston Glock developed his first pistol in response to an RFP from the Austrian Army, which had previously awarded Glock a contract to produce a military shovel using polymers to lighten the weight of the tool without compromising its strength.

Military planners have always been concerned about the amount of weight that a trooper carries in the field. The greater the weight carried, the less mobility and the quicker the soldier gets tired out. The weight of the soldier's gun will also impact the weight of the ammunition which must be carried because the less ammunition available to reload the gun, the less effective will be the trooper's performance in the field.

This thinking was paramount in the mind of America's second important gun designer (after John Browning) named Eugene Stoner, who designed a new military rifle, known as the AR, in 1955. This gun, which would replace the standard-issue M-14, weighed 6 pounds, 9 ounces, whereas the M-14 weighed in at 8.3 pounds. The M-14 was the first full-auto military rifle carried by U. S. troops, having been developed in the 1950's to replace the venerable M-1, which General Patton had called, "the greatest battle implement ever devised."

18

The M-14, like the M-1, was chambered for a 30-caliber round, which had been the standard military load since before World War I. The limitation of the M-1, however, was its top-loading design, which meant the gun could only hold 8-9 rounds because the magazine could not be too large, or it would stick out above the frame and impede the ability of the shooter to aim the gun.

The M-14 was both full-automatic and also loaded from beneath the frame. But the size and weight of the ammunition reduced its effectiveness because the trooper using such a gun would quickly expend all his ammunition unless he was willing to carry more ammunition which would only wear him down.

Enter Gene Stoner with a lightweight, bottom-loading, full-auto gun which shot a 22-caliber, high-powered round known as the .223. The diameter of the shell was the same size as the sporting, 22LR caliber, but the amount of powder in the case would drive the round twice as fast as the 22LR cartridge, and a trooper could carry twice as many .223 rounds with the same or less weight than the 30-caliber ammunition used in the M-14.

Stoner's polymer gun was issued to the United States military at the same time that Gaston Glock was developing his polymer-based handgun. As soon as these types of weapons were issued to the military, civilian models were produced for sale to retail gun customers in the United States.

Let's pause for a moment in our technical discussion and return to a consideration of mass shooting events.

On August 1, 1966, an ex-Marine named Charles Whitman, first stabbed his mother to death in her Austin, Texas home, then went back to his house where he stabbed his wife to death. Approximately 12 hours after Whitman killed his wife, at 11:30 A.M. he entered the main campus of the University of Texas at Austin, climbed up to the 28th floor of the observation tower and began shooting at human targets below.

Before Whitman was gunned down by an Austin cop some 90 minutes after his rampage began, he had killed 3 people in the tower, then shot 11 more from his perch and wounded some 30 others, many of whom were more than 500 feet away from where Whitman sat and aimed his gun. Most of his victims were killed by a scoped, Remington bolt-action in 6mm, a rifle not very different than the one used by another former Marine who assassinated a President from an elevated location in 1963.

Whitman's mass assault was not the first time that someone with a gun had attempted to murder multiple people located within the same, public space. In 1903 a military veteran fired into a crowd in Winfield, KS, killing 9 and wounding 25 others who were assembled for a concert performed by the town band. The shooter also died but whether it was a suicide or someone responding with lethal force has never been solved.

Whitman used a hunting rifle for his attack. The veteran, Gilbert Twigg, who fired into the crowd in Winfield, emerged from an alleyway and used a shotgun for his assault. These types of guns, bolt-action rifles and pump-action shotguns are still sold and make up a large percentage of all the guns found in American homes. But they are not the types of guns used in mass shootings today.

Yet notwithstanding the recent mass assaults in Uvalde, Buffalo, and Highland Park, one shouldn't make the mistake of thinking that the assault rifle, otherwise referred to as the AR-15, is always the mass shooter's weapon of choice.

The greatest number of fatal casualties suffered in any mass shooting before 49 were killed at a nightclub in Orlando on June 12, 2016, and 60 people were killed at a Las Vegas rock concert in 2017, took place at Virginia Tech University on April 16, 2007, when a 23-year-old senior, Seung Hui-Cho, killed 32 students and faculty members before taking his own life. The shooter used a Glock pistol, almost the same gun which another mass shooter, Elliot Rodger used when he drove around the college town of Santa Isla, CA, killing and wounding 10 people before taking his own life on May 23, 2014.

The advantages of using an assault rifle instead of a pistol to commit mass murder are as follows: (1). Even in semi-auto mode, you can deliver a lot of firepower to the scene. At Sandy Hook, the shooter discharged more than 90 rounds in 3 minutes or less. (2). The rifle is lightweight, easily carried and can be moved from one position to another without the shooter losing point-of-aim. (3). With a 16-inch barrel and retractable stock, the gun can easily be hidden under a raincoat or some other outerwear.

Let's say, however, for the sake of argument, that the shooter feels more comfortable using a handgun rather than any kind of longer and bigger gun. If the gun is a semi-automatic, bottom-loading pistol, it can easily be hidden in a pocket or a small bag. Bring along 3 or 4 more loaded magazines and you are entering the shooting area with 60-75 lethal rounds which the U.S. Army has decided are lethal enough to be issued to our troops since 1975.

These are the reasons why, tactically speaking, polymer handguns and long guns are now used in virtually every mass shooting which occurs in the United States. But there is one more reason why such guns are purchased more frequently than any other type of weapon by individuals who want to use a gun to commit multiple homicides or want to carry a gun for self-protection inside and outside the house, or just have an impulse to go into a gun shop or go to the website of an online gun dealer and buy a gun.

And the reason has to do with the most important issue of all when it comes to understanding why mass shootings occur so frequently in the United States, namely the degree to which the companies that manufacture guns derive about twice the profit from a polymer-based gun than a gun made from carbon or alloyed steels. Consequently, contemporary marketing narratives used by gun companies to sell their products, overwhelmingly focus on polymer-based guns.

Which takes us to the next chapter, where we explain the economics of the gun business in the United States.

CHAPTER 2. THE ECONOMICS OF MASS SHOOTINGS.

Want to make a million dollars in the gun business? Start with two million.

My great-uncle Ben, who manufactured a cheap Saturday Night Special back in the old days, used to make that comment to me all the time. His gun, which was a 22-caliber revolver, cost about $15 to make, he then sold it to local pawn shops for $25 and they marked it up to $30 or $35.

The gun worked once. The cylinder was a piece of pressed steel, so it fell apart when the gun was shot for the first time. When the government passed the big gun-control law in 1968 which set manufacturing standards to prevent cheap, foreign-made guns from coming into the domestic market, Uncle Ben's gun also fell by the wayside and Uncle Ben became a law enforcement wholesaler for Smith & Wesson.

The economics of the gun business have changed since those days, but they haven't changed all that much. It is still a business with slim margins and the constant threat of excess inventory, the latter condition caused by the simple fact that guns happen to be a consumer item which consumers don't really need, and which don't wear out.

Guns were considered an essential household item when we were opening and settling our frontier. But according to the Census, the frontier ceased to exist in 1890. The disappearance of a frontier environment not only meant that we didn't need to defend ourselves against human threats, such as attacks from Native American tribes or highwaymen and the like.

23

It also meant that we didn't need to engage in hunting in order to secure necessary food.

The fact that many Americans continued to own guns in the twentieth century was as much out of habit as anything else. Indeed, even the uniformed services who carry guns today rarely need to use those guns in carrying out their daily, peacekeeping tasks. And as more and more of the population lives away from rural zones, so the ownership of guns in the more urbanized and suburbanized zones continues to decline.

It has been estimated that guns could be found in 40% of American households in the 1970's, a percentage which has dropped down to somewhere around 25% today. Since the total population has increased from roughly 200 million in 1970 to slightly above 330 million in 2020, this means that in raw numbers, there were roughly 80 million gun-owning households in 1970 and there are still roughly 80 million gun-owning households today.

But here is where we get into the second problem facing the gun industry, namely, the problem of excess inventory, which is what makes it so easy to start off with two million dollars and end up with one million bucks. Because the problem is that guns don't wear out. If a gun is designed and manufactured to withstand the extreme pressures generated by the discharge of a shell, that gun will continue to function for decades with only minimum care.

I own a Colt 1911 pistol that was first shipped out of the Colt factory in Hartford in 1923. Along with the gun, I also have 20 rounds of 45acp ammunition made by the Remington ammunition factory in Bridgeport that was sold as a promotion with the gun. Actually, I only have 17 rounds of the ammunition because I used 3 rounds to test fire the gun. Both the gun and the ammunition work just fine.

Meanwhile, the factory where Colt manufactured the gun in Hartford has been vacant for years, the Bridgeport factory where Remington made the ammunition is rubble. I often drive past both factories when I come down from my home in Massachusetts to visit friends or family in New York. The Colt factory sits empty alongside I-91, the shell of the Remington factory is next to I-95.

How long will the car last that I drive past those two buildings which turned out my still-functioning Colt1911 pistol and its ammunition a century ago? If I'm lucky, I'll get seven or eight years out of the car.

When did I last trade in my handheld phone? Two years ago, when I moved my monthly plan from Verizon to AT&T. When did I purchase the laptop which I'm using to write this text in July 2022? I replaced the previous laptop last month which I bought in 2019.

I need a laptop, I need a cell, I need a car. I don't need any of the more than 20 guns I have lying in various closets and underneath various beds in my house. I have another 40 personally owned guns down in my gun shop. I don't need any of them, either.

Why do I have all these guns? Because I like guns. When was the last time I bought a gun? Sometime last month. I probably buy a gun every couple of months.

So, if I buy many more guns than laptops or droids, how come the gun industry has to worry about inventory stacking up on the factory or gun shop shelves? Please read the next sentence very, very carefully, okay?

Just about every time I go out and buy another gun to add to my collection, I also get rid of a gun. Because guns don't break down with minimum care, they also retain their value and thus allow me to acquire a gun without dispensing a lot of cash. Walk into the typical gun shop and you'll discover that maybe half the guns in the dealer's inventory did not come from a gun factory or a gun wholesaler. They came from someone like me who used a gun already owned to acquire a 'new' gun.

Every month the FBI publishes a report on how many background checks for gun purchases were performed by the FBI-UCR phone bank in West Virginia, which is an office complex right off of I-79, about ten miles south of Morgantown. To the dismay of all the gun-control groups, the monthly number of background checks jumped alarmingly in 2020 and 2021, due most likely to fears about Covid-19.

Not one expert who raised this issue in the media ever mentioned that there was absolutely no way to determine whether any background check represented a new gun coming into the civilian arsenal or was a previously owned gun moving from one owner to the next.

The gun business is a unique type of economic structure because it remains the only two-tiered merchandising system which moves products from where they are made to where they are sold but still requires the intervention of a middle party called a wholesaler who is the initial purchaser of virtually all newly manufactured guns.

When I was a kid in the 1950's, I sometimes went with my grandfather to the Washington Street market in lower Manhattan where he would select and pay for the fresh fruits and vegetables that would be delivered to his grocery store later that day. We would walk around the market at 5 a.m., then leave and get back to the store at 6 a.m., then open the store and wait for the truck which brought the fresh goods that Grandpa would sell later that day and the next several days.

This area in lower Manhattan was known as the 'wholesale district,' and in the 1950's there were still wholesale companies operating out of warehouses and lofts on Chambers Street, Murray Street, Warren

Street and several other streets between Broadway and Greenwich Streets, just a little bit to the west of City Hall.

These wholesale enterprises were still shipping household goods and hardware products to retailers all over the United States, particularly retail establishments in smaller cities and towns located in the South and the farm belt of the Midwest. Many of these wholesale operations hung on even when the entire neighborhood began to change with the construction of the two towers of the World Trade Center which went up in the early 1970's and came down in 2001.

By the time the WTC was attacked, however, the wholesale neighborhood had disappeared, largely because of the appearance and proliferation of mass-market, big-box chain stores, as well as new technologies for moving staples and consumer goods around the globe.

The town where I now live in Western Massachusetts used to have two hardware stores, one of which was also a small lumber yard. Both these stores closed the day that a Home Depot opened up next to the Wal Mart, who's opening a year earlier produced the closure of two, family-owned clothing stores. The two drug stores, a Walgreens, and a CVS, are also national chains.

These stores all purchase their inventories directly from the companies which manufacture those goods. Many of these factories are located overseas but orders which are received in China or India can be drop-shipped by air freight into the United States within a couple of days. This international movement of goods is what also stocks the cute, little clothing boutiques in the college town near where I live. The blueberries I purchased yesterday at Stop and Shop came from Peru, and I don't mean Peru, Indiana or Peru, Illinois.

This consolidation of the supply chain for consumer goods has not, for the most part, occurred with guns. First, there is the licensing issue, which requires that every company which touches a new gun from the factory to the retail point-of-sale must be licensed and open for inspection by the ATF. Second, and perhaps more important, is the liability and risk to a sales operation represented by guns, particularly handguns.

Some of the big-box stores which stock sporting goods like Wal Mart and Dick's, will sell long guns over the counter and often run specials on ammunition when the hunting season starts up. But these stores do not sell handguns or assault rifles, which happen to be the revenue and profit drivers for the gun makers, an issue we will discuss in detail below.

Finally, and this is perhaps the most important reason gun commerce at the retail point of sale remains so localized and concentrated in small, independently owned stores. This reflects the nature or what we might call the culture of gun retailing, something not understood at all by the media 'experts' who write about guns.

First, what we call the 20-80 rule in merchandising, which says that 20 percent of the retailers sell 80% of the consumer goods, is nowhere more extreme than in the gun business, where the ratio of large to small retailers is probably more in the area of 90-10. Most gun shops are owned by retired gun nuts whose wives at some point told them to take all the 'gun crap' out of the house and rent a little storefront in the town. Not only does this decision get the old man out of the house each day, but it also makes space in the house for much-needed consumer junk that the wife wants around.

My gun shop is located in a town of roughly 11,000 residents. The three closest towns to my town are all located about ten miles away, they all have around 10,000 residents and each town has a gun shop where the proprietor is at least 60 years old and started the shop with inventory that he had acquired over the years.

I once did a study of the zip codes of the previous several hundred customers who bought guns in my shop. The information was available on the 4473 forms which must be filled out by the customer in order for the dealer to conduct a background check. More than 90% of the customers who bought guns in my shop came from zip codes which were less than 20 miles away from me. In order to get to my shop, every one of these customers had to drive past at least one other gun shop.

Did these guys stop at the other shop or maybe two shops before they came to my shop? Of course, they did. And when they walked into my shop and asked how much credit they would get for some old, piece of junk which they wanted to trade on another piece of used junk which was displayed on a shelf in my store, they would always tell me that so-and-so in the gun shop down the road had offered them 'more.'

Every year the ATF publishes a list of the names and addresses of every federally licensed gun dealer in the United States. The moment the list is published, the gun-control organizations send out funding appeals lamenting about the 60,000-gun dealers who have 'blood on their hands,' or some other such inflammatory remark.

The idea that there are some 60,000 Americans engaged in the act of buying and selling retail guns is not only wrong, but also so wrong that I cannot think of another consumer product category which abounds with such narratives so far removed from the truth.

Someone who applies for and receives a federal firearms license (FFL) is not required to engage in anything having to do with the gun business at all. Even if the licensed individual identifies a commercial or business address om his license, it can be a location where he does something other than deal in guns. I know three FFL holders in my town who have never sold a gun to anyone but themselves.

Why do these guys and thousands of guys just like them go to the trouble of getting a federal gun license and then renewing it every three years? Because the cost of that license is significantly less than what they would pay me or another gun retailer for a gun since with their FFL they can buy guns directly from gun factories or gun wholesalers. When the gun arrives, they call the FBI in West Virginia, do a background check on themselves, transfer the gun from their dealer's inventory to their own state-issued gun license (if they live in a state which even bothers to issue a license to own guns) and now they personally own another gun.

When the gun-control research group at Harvard did a study in 2015 which showed that guns were increasingly owned by a smaller and smaller percentage of households, a study which shocked all the right-minded people in the gun-control community, the research team neglected to ask the gun owners who were identified as owning, on average, between eight and one hundred guns, whether or not they held federal gun licenses either as dealers or collectors.

Notwithstanding the gun industry's effort to promote sales based on the idea that owning a gun is a necessity in a fearsome world where threats abound, the average gun owner is basically a hobbyist whose hobby involves using guns either for occasional sport shooting or hunting, or just sitting on the couch and playing with one of his guns. The gun industry has tried every type of sales and marketing messaging to break out of a reliance on older, White males in smaller cities and towns to form a more diverse population that would want to own guns, and these initiatives have failed every, single time.

How do you maintain or increase profit margins when you are selling products into a static market whose size, relatively speaking, doesn't change in a positive way? The industry's response to this problem has been to reduce the costs of making their products, which explains how and why polymer-based guns have become the guns of choice.

Before polymer started to be used as the basic material for producing guns, every handgun and long gun started out as a chunk of carbon steel or alloyed steel. The chunk was melted down, poured into a mold, which then became part of the gun's frame. Depending on the gun's design, the frame would consist of multiple pieces, which after the hardened and were removed from the molds would be polished and then fitted together to form the gun's frame.

The gun's frame contained the moveable parts which were used to fire the gun – trigger, hammer, slide in pistols, cylinder in revolvers, bolts in rifles and shotguns, springs which connected the moving parts. Along with the frame, the barrel and the grips, a revolver's frame would usually contain some 25 individual parts, a semi-auto pistol might contain 30-35 individual parts, a semi-auto rifle frame would also contain 30-35 parts.

Before the pieces which formed the gun's frame were locked together with screws that connected the two sides, each piece needed to be carefully polished so that there would be an exact fit with no chance of the frame loosening up because of recoil pressures released when the gun was shot. After the frame was completely assembled, its sides had to be polished so that a finish could be applied to the surface to protect the gun from rusting or otherwise becoming discolored or damaged by water or chemicals that might spill on the gun.

After the finish was applied to the gun by immersing the frame in a hot solution of chemicals and acids, the frame would be dried and polished again. Once all of this work was completed, all the internal parts and springs would be fitted inside the gun's frame, and then it would be taken out to the test range and fired several times to check both the functioning of all the parts as well as the barrel's placement and aim.

Even though we talk about the gun industry as having pioneered the modern Industrial Revolution through a reliance on the assembly line and the use of interchangeable parts, in fact if one were to walk through a gun factory before the advent of injection-molding polymer along with M2M (metal-to-metal) technologies, what you would have seen were a bunch of small, craft-based activities operating under one roof.

What used to be the major cost of gun manufacturing, the labor required to make, polish, finish, and fit guns, has completely disappeared and has been replaced by materials and technologies which have reduced the cost of gun making to a fraction of what the cost used to be. In 1978, Smith & Wesson's Springfield workforce numbered slightly more than 2,000 men and women who produced somewhere around 400,000 guns. In 2020, with a workforce that was still slightly above 2,000 employees, the company manufactured 1.2 million guns.

Guns with polymer frames are not only smaller and stronger than guns made out of carbon steel, but they also need minimum upkeep and maintenance to avoid surface blemishes or rust. In the pre-polymer days, it was not unusual to walk into a gun owner's home and find him sitting in his easy chair in the living room or the den with a rag and a can of oil, polishing his guns.

When Glock started marketing their guns in the United States during the 1980's, one of their ads showed a pistol sitting in a pool of muddy water, then picked up by the owner who would shoot of a few rounds without even first wiping off the gun. I had trouble getting my first Glock licensed by the NYPD because those gun experts decided that the gun was entirely made out of plastic and therefore could be brought through a metal detector and snuck into a courtroom or taken on a plane.

When I told the NYPD gun inspector that the pistol couldn't be shot without a barrel and the barrel had to be made out of steel, he shrugged and said he wasn't going to approve the gun for my personal use anyway. After all, why say 'yes' when it's just as easy to say 'no?' The standard NYPD duty weapon issued to all officers today happens to be a Glock.

Would mass shootings which kill and injure twenty, thirty or forty adults and children be as common in the United States if Americans didn't have access to polymer-based guns? Let's put it this way. Someone who is determined to commit mass murder will try to find some way to accomplish this task, easy or not. The moment that such a person begins to contemplate a mass killing event by using something other than a rapid-fire gun, the logistical issues become significant and extreme.

Between 1978 and 1995, Ted Kaczynski, also known as the 'Unabomber,' sent or tried to send 15 explosive devices to various locations throughout the United States. He ended up injuring a dozen individuals and killing three. Bombs may have killed and injured many more victims, such as the bomb planted by the Tsarnaev Brothers at the finish line of the Boston Marathon in 2013 which killed 3 persons but injured several hundred more. But going about constructing a bomb that will actually work is a much more involved and complicated effort than simply acquiring a gun.

When someone walks into a crowded theater, or a jammed nightclub, or even a classroom in an elementary school and starts spraying a gun all over the place, if nothing else this behavior represents what is at that moment a very impulsive act. This impulsiveness was brought home to me in a conversation I had with a police officer in Tulsa, Oklahoma, following the fatal shooting of the owner of s small barber shop.

This incident took place in 2015 in the Gifted Hands Barber Shop. The victim was the shop owner, Keith Liggins, who was considered something of a community leader in Tulsa's Black community and the shop was often the site of unofficial gatherings for members of the community who wanted to discuss neighborhood issues or just sit around, chat a bit and relax. One evening, while Liggins was cutting a patron's hair, two young men rushed into the shop. One of them was holding an AK-47 rifle and began spraying rounds all over the place.

Their target was another young man who was sitting in a chair waiting to get his hair cut. He wasn't hit by any of the AK-47 rounds, but the barber took a round through his head and dopped dead. The young man sitting in the chair pulled a handgun out of his pocket and fired a shot at the kid holding the AK-47, the latter individual and his friend retreated out of the shop and were arrested the next day.

Several weeks after this shooting, which created a community-wide anger because the barber was someone whom everyone respected and liked, I had a conversation with one of the Tulsa cops who worked on this case. He was a twelve-year veteran of the Tulsa PD, and he had been a member of the street crime – homicide unit for several years.

I asked him how come the shooter with the AK-47 sprayed ammunition all over the shop when he interested in only assaulting one particular individual who was seated at least ten feet asway from the man who ended getting shot.

Here was his answer: "That's how it always happens. They never shoot the gun once or twice. They pull the trigger again and again until there's no more ammunition left in the gun."

To fully understand the economics of the gun business, which promotes guns made with polymer which end up as the kinds of guns used in mass shootings, one must be sensitive to the extent that impulsiveness is the behavioral factor which must be taken into account to understand what mass shootings all are about.

People buy guns out of impulse. People pull these guns out and point them at someone out of impulse, or to quote Lester Adelson, a gun is "what converts a spat into a slaying and a quarrel into a killing." And even if someone spends month carefully preparing and planning a shooting in many victims end up on the hospital or the morgue, the moment when the gun is pointed at those human targets and the trigger is pulled, is still an impulsive act.

The gun industry is aware of the impulsive behavior which produces the physical harm created by the use of its products. The next chapter will discuss how media messaging created by the gun industry, captures this impulsive behavior and channels it into mass shooting events.

3. PROMOTING MASS SHOOTING GUNS.

In June or July 1971, I was working for my Uncle Ben who was the Smith & Wesson law enforcement wholesaler for South Carolina and had a nice warehouse and retail store down the road from the headquarters of the State Police. As I mentioned in the previous chapter, I had worked for Ben in his North Carolina gun factory in the mid-1960's when he made a cheap, 22-caliber handgun that was prohibited to be produced by the federal gun law passed in 1968. So, instead of making his own gun, Ben sold guns made by Smith & Wesson to the cops and everyone else.

One day during my time in Ben's shop, three or four retail customers walked in and asked to buy a Model 29. This was a blued, six-inch barrel revolver that S&W had been manufacturing since 1955, which was chambered for the 44-msgum cartridge and packed a wallop every time it was shot. If you shot it quickly more than three times, your ears were ringing, and your hands felt like they were going to fall off.

Maybe we sold two of these guns every year, maybe three. If we weren't required to keep at least one model of every S&W gun in the inventory, we probably wouldn't have stocked it at all. So how come three different customers walked into the shop on the same day and wanted to buy the gun?

After the third customer departed emptyhanded, I picked up the phone, called the factory and spoke to Del Shorb. He was the sporting goods Vice President for S&W, and even though his division sold a lot more guns than the law enforcement side under

Dave Simons, it was Smith & Wesson's near-monopoly of sales to cops which was the primary promoter of the company brand.

For that reason, I figured Dave would be happy to ship me down a couple of Model 29 handguns. Except to my great surprise, he told me that he was 'completely cleaned out' of the gun and because he hadn't anticipated the demand, didn't figure to getting the gun restocked for at least another three to four months.

Smith & Wesson missed a great opportunity to add to its bottom line because this was the first time that a gun was not just used in a Hollywood movie, but occupied center stage in the movie's plot. After all, I was raised on cowboy movies which featured either the cavalry mowing down Indians with their Winchester saddle rifles, or a lone gunfighter like Shane using a revolver to go up against a bad guy and even the score.

But Dirty Harry was different because not only did Clint use the gun with abandon in the San Francisco streets, but he made a point of saying that his gun was the 'most powerful' and the 'most effective' gun around. If you had a Smith & Wesson Model 29, you weren't just walking around with a handgun, you were walking around with the most unique handgun that money could buy.

From that time onward, American box-office movie hits usually portrayed two motifs. First, the movies contained frequent, explicit, and graphic violent scenes. The violence was not only the handiwork of the movie's lead, but invariably the violence was used by the movie's lead actor (both male and female) to advance a specific cause or achieve a specific result. A study of 390 top-grossing movies released between 1985 and 2010 found that violence, defined as "intentional acts (e.g., to cause harm, to coerce, or for fun) where the aggressor makes or attempts to make some physical contact that has potential to inflict injury or harm." occurred in nearly 90% of all top-grossing films.

Along with an increasing use of violence to build film audience and box-office revenues, Hollywood productions began to choose specific types and models of guns, aided in this regard by some gun manufacturers who saw movies as an effective way to strengthen their brands. The most aggressive gun maker in this respect was Glock, which first began to move large numbers of its handgun production into the American consumer market, particularly after opening an American subsidiary in Georgia in 1986.

Glock not only offered moviemakers free samples of their guns to use in their productions, but also recognized the market exposure for their products in video shooting games, which generates billions of dollars in annual revenues, a number that has increased exponentially over the past decade as video gaming of all kinds has moved from stationary game boxes to social media streamed through handheld devices.

One should not make the mistake, however, of assuming that mass shooting and shooting behavior are promoted primarily by video games that are played either in groups or by individuals on computers, game boxes or TV. Even though a shooting extravaganza like Modern Warfare generates almost $2 billion in annual revenues, shooting electronic impulses at moving targets have been popular all the way back to the days of video arcades.

What we are talking about in this chapter is the shift of products in the gun business and related businesses from hunting and sport shooting to military and tactical motifs which began in the 1990's, prior to 9/11 and the War on Terror and emerged as a full-blown cultural and fashion statement beginning with the Gulf War and Desert Storm in 1990-1991.

I encountered tactical culture for the first time when I attended a fundraiser in the home of an Orthodox Jewish man that was deep in the bowels of the deeply Orthodox Brooklyn neighborhood of Williamsburg. I accompanied a friend who was a professional fundraiser for various Orthodox social service organizations, in this case a children's health program which allegedly existed in the Orthodox neighborhood in Israel known as Bnei Brak.

This is a town of some two square miles located on the border of Jerusalem where you aren't allowed to drive a car on any of its streets from sundown Friday night until the Sabbath ends the following night. The men walk around wearing traditional, ultra-religious clothing like those big, fur-lined hats, and the women wear skirts down to their ankles and are always surrounded by a lot of kids.

Since Williamsburg is part of New York City, the rules for public behavior are somewhat less strict, but go into the home of one of these religious families and you're no longer in the modern world, or at least the way most people define the word 'modern,' which means defining your everyday behavior by the norms embraced by the larger society, as opposed to following the strictures of the Old Testament, word for word.

The man who hosted the fundraising event had been told that I was a gun guy, so he took me out to his backyard and gave me a tour inside what had been a two-car garage but had been converted into a small workshop where several Chinese women were running sewing machines non-stop. They were making tactical pants out of some kind of camouflage-colored material which the proprietor proudly showed me matched up to military-type shirts which even had the little cell=phone pockets on the sleeve.

As I said above, this was 1990 or 1991. Cell phones were popular, but they weren't *that* popular just yet. Droids didn't exist. What we now call tactical gear – boots, gloves, tools and other military and cop equipment was only sold in shops that stocked uniforms - there were maybe three such establishments in all of New York City – or in Army-Navy stores which basically sold second-hand clothing to kids. My son, who was a year away from high school, hung out in an Army-Navy store near his school which sold pirated movie cassettes from under the counter if you knew how to ask.

The guy in Williamsburg told me that he was making a 'fortune' selling the tactical outfits to a K-Mart store. He was thinking of taking a booth at the upcoming national trade show for the gun industry, the SHOT show, which was going to be held that year in Orlando, a city where my host, as he told me, could easily buy orthodox, Kosher food.

By the mid-1990's, tactical clothing, tactical gear, and tactical guns were all over the place. In other words, to all intents and purposes, tactical had become mainstream, and not just a fashion statement adopted by people who owned guns. What this meant for the gun industry was an important cross-over between products which brought consumers into places where guns were sold (i.e., guns) and products which gun owners might be tempted to purchase even if such purchases weren't guns.

Recall that Chapter 2 started with the joke about making a million dollars in the gun business by starting with two million. At best, the profit margin at the retail point-of-sale for guns has never been more than 20 percent. The retail margin for ammunition is maybe 30 percent, which is more or less the margin for optics and other accessory items that often go out the shop door with a gun.

Clothing, on the other hand, often has a retail margin of 50 percent, and if a store purchases and pays for the clothing inventory the day the shipment arrives, rather than waiting until the '30 days net' date hits, the discount becomes wider still. Before tactical clothing started to appear, at best a gun shop might sell a camo shirt and an orange vest in the month before the deer season began. Tactical clothing, however, sells year-round.

Along with the guns and the clothing, another accessory area which developed through the growth in tactical interest was optics, in particular sighting aids that could be mounted on assault rifles to give these guns a more military style and look. Gun owners who used their guns for hunting usually added a fixed or variable scope at a cost of several hundred dollars, prices which fell as these optics increasingly were manufactured in Far East factories on the Pacific Rim.

The scopes that were promoted with tactical guns, however, were often advertised as being military 'grade,' which meant they would stand up even if the gun on which the scope was mounted was dropped or otherwise physically abused. Tactical weapons also began to come with lasers or bright lights for night-time use, even though not one of the 50 states allowed for hunting after dark.

If a consumer walked into a gun shop to purchase a new, bolt-action hunting rifle manufactured by Ruger, Remington, or Savage Arms, he could expect to spend $600 on the gun, another $200 for a scope, $20 for a sling, and perhaps another $40 for a soft case, as well as $20 for 20 rounds of ammunition. A first-rate hunting package would cost around $900, give, or take a few.

If instead or in addition to a hunting gun, someone wanted to get into the tactical thing, the gun would cost $800, the optics another $400, a tactical sling would be $50, a mat which would allow the shooter to lie prone would cost another $75, the carrying case might be a hard case because it needed to be battle-resistant and that would be another $75, plus the ammunition – total for the package could easily run $1,400.

When tactical products first started being produced, the gun industry did some promotions showing shooters in tactical clothing, up to and including their faces being darkened, sitting in a tree, and obviously using their tactical weapons for hunting, as if a deer wouldn't smell the shooter because he was dressed in camo, black and dark green.

Very quickly the gun industry abandoned this rather silly effort to move the hunting population into becoming tactical shooters, if only because hunters usually tended to be versant on what they needed to bring into the field for a hunt, and what they didn't need was a military-style gun shooting ammunition that was designed to be used in tactical situations in which the targets were humans, not animals.

To help strengthen the product shift from hunting to tactical guns, the industry invented an entirely new definition and name for assault rifles, dropping the nomenclature which surrounded the word 'tactical' and replacing it with the word 'sporting,' as in 'modern sporting gun.' The idea here was to use the idea of 'sport' to replace the idea of 'tactical' and shift popular gun culture away from the military application of weapons to a more benign, sporting point of view.

The attempt to fuse sporting and tactical product worlds together could only go so far, however, because there was just too much of a financial incentive occasioned by tactical products to allow for the focus to be on sport. The fact that the gun industry was increasingly reliant on handgun sales, particularly handguns which were promoted as products that were essential for self-defense, made it all the more reason why guns that were primarily non-sporting in design and use would drive the types of products being advertised and sold.

Here is a typical advertisement for a self-defense handgun from Springfield Arms:

Note the promotion which gives the buyer of a Springfield handgun a range bag, along with extra mags. Note the expression – 'gear up.' The word 'gear' came into the gun glossary as a reflection of the shift towards tactical products in general and specifically as the industry promoted tactical-style guns. Hunters didn't carry gear, soldiers carried gear.

You would think that even if many Americans felt that carrying a personal-defense handgun was a rational response to concerns or fears about crime, that the need to be armed both inside and outside the home wouldn't extend itself to tactical guns or tactical gear. After all, think what you might about 9-11 and other real or potential terrorist threats, the United States is still thousands of miles away from countries whose military could conceivably come ashore in California or some East Coast state and transform this country into a battle zone.

The way that gun companies market the guns that are used in mass shootings, however, you would think that sooner or later everyone who keeps an assault rifle in their home will have to take their gun and assemble in a civilian militia to help drive the invaders out.

Here's an advertisement run by Daniel Defense, a manufacturer of the assault rifle that was used in mass shootings in 2022 that killed and injured more than 30 victims in Buffalo, New York and Uvalde, Texas., over a span of just 10 days:

It is perhaps understandable that gun companies will promote their products by connecting their products up with the way such items are used in real life. Back in the 1950's, for example, gun companies like Winchester often ran illustrated ads for their rifles which featured scenes and backdrops out of the Old West:

It would be one thing if it were the case that selling the guns which are used in mass shootings were pictured as being necessary to help protect us from military or terrorist threats. As unreal as that narrative would be, at least it would exhibit some degree of reality in terms of the history and development of the M-16 and its civilian version, the AR-15.

Here is a typical assault rifle advertisement from Mossberg Firearms which neatly combines a description of the gun's engineering with an appeal to the country's core values of patriotism and the American way:

What the gun industry has done to promote sales of assault rifles, however, is to move beyond appeals to America's political culture and focus more specifically on the psychological impulses of younger males who often look for ways to advance their feelings of self-esteem by seeing themselves as being stronger and tougher than their peers.

The battle rifles that were supplied to troops in both world wars were manufactured in the government arsenal in Springfield where slightly more than 3.5 million guns were manufactured between 1932 and 1945. Production was resumed during the Korean War when another 600,000 rifles were turned out.

Between 1941 and 1945, the M-1 was also produced under government contract at the Winchester Repeating Arms factory in Connecticut, and additional guns were produced at the factories of Harrington & Richardson in Massachusetts and International Harvester in Indiana during and just after the Korean War.

At no point did any of these gunmakers produce weapons for commercial sale, even though as semi-automatic weapons there was no legal reason why such guns would have been considered too dangerous or lethal for civilians to own. The first full-auto gun produced for the U.S. military was the M-14, which went into service in 1959 and replaced the M-1. Like the M-1 it was manufactured at the Springfield arsenal plus contracts were given by the government to Harrington & Richardson and Winchester Repeating Arms.

Like the M-1, the M-14 was never manufactured for any non-government recipient and was not sold off as a surplus weapon the way that the M-1 started moving into the civilian market after it was decommissioned for military use. This difference between military and civilian gun manufacture changed, however, when the government closed the Springfield Arsenal in 1968 and began sourcing out production of military guns to private contractors, beginning with the first M-16 contract that was given to Colt Firearms in Hartford, CT.

Colt was previously the primary manufacturer of the M1911 pistol which the Army and then other branches of the military began adopting in 19111. But this gun, which was manufactured at the Colt factory in Hartford, was no different from the 1911 pistol which Colt began selling to the civilian market at the same time that it was shipping the military model to Army units just prior to World War I.

The Colt company was the first of many private gun makers to manufacture the 1911 pistol for both military and commercial sales, a practice which broke down the distinction between military and non-military gun production which existed until the Springfield Arsenal was closed down in 1968. The only difference between the military and civilian models of the rifle was the replacement of the auto sear with a semi-auto sear, the part which controlled whether the gun would fire in full-auto or semi-auto mode. Otherwise, the M-16 and the AR-15 rifles were the same gun.

Even the difference between he fully-automatic military rifle and the semi-automatic civilian gun could be circumvented by the use of a part known as a bump stock, whose attachment to the semi-automatic gun's stock allowed a shooter to fire his semi-automatic gun in full-auto mode, which is how the shooter who killed 60 people and injured hundreds more was able to fire 1,000-plus rounds at the crowd attending a rock concert on October 1, 2017.

As of March 26, 2019, the ownership of a bump stock device must be cleared through the same NFA licensing process that is required for the ownership of any full-auto gun. Nevertheless, attaching a home-made bump stock to a semi-automatic AR-15 is easily accomplished and can even be done by using a leather belt instead of a solid gun stock.

YouTube used to have videos which showed how to assemble and attach a home-made bump stock, content which they banned from the site after the ATF published its new rule. But such videos circulate throughout the digital world, particularly on the hundreds of Facebook and Reddit gun groups which attract thousands of viewers online.

Whenever a shooting occurs which generates media interest and the gun used in the shooting is identified, sale of that particular gun tend to go up. In fact, the FBI does not break down specific types of gun models for which background checks occur, except to note three basic categories: handguns, long guns, and 'other' guns. In June 2022 one month after the Uvalde and Buffalo shootings, background checks for 'other' guns were the highest number recorded in that category since June 2009, when that separate designation was added to the monthly FBI/UCR background check report.

What does the word 'other' gun mean It is a serialized receiver or lower frame without an attached barrel, so it qualifies as a gun that can only be sold following a background check, but without a barrel it cannot be classified as either a handgun or a long gun. One of the reasons that assault rifles have become so popular is that they are easily put together without requiring special tools and their hands-on construction is similar to what folks did with ham radios back in the 1960's before desktop computers came along.

There has yet to be a single research effort which has attempted to ask people why they run out to buy a certain type of gun after the weapon is identified as having been used in a high-profile shooting, particularly a mass shooting where many people are injured or killed.

I have my own theory about this issue, but it will wait until the end of the book.

4. MILITIAS AND MASS SHOOTINGS.

The militia movement became a media issue when it was first reported that Timothy McVeigh had spent some time with the Michigan Militia before going down to Oklahoma City and blowing up the Murrah Federal Building, which was the worst act of domestic terrorism until the Twin Towers attacks in 2001.

Nobody knows how many members are actively enrolled in militia groups, nor do we even know exactly how many of these groups exist in the present day. The Southern Poverty Law Center has identified some 300 groups, but the SPLC has a tendency to see an extreme, right-wing political group under every bed, so to speak.

The Anti-Defamation League claims that current militia group numbers are in excess of 500 groups, but like the SPLC, the ADL also tends to exaggerate the size and danger posed by right-wing extremist activities. Several years ago, I visited the two locations in Boston which the ADL claimed were sites that housed Nazi groups. One location was a small, basement bookshop that was closed, the other was an Army-Navy store which sold a few pieces of Nazi memorabilia.

In 1991 or 1992 I spent a day with the Michigan Militia at a shooting range and picnic grove where the group was holding its monthly meet. The members were, for the most part, men in their 40's and 50's who spent the day basically socializing with one another, shooting their guns, eating pizza, and drinking plenty of beer. In other words, a fun time was had by all.

In fact, the Michigan Militia had evidently become less military-minded and more concerned with what they referred to as 'community awareness and preparedness' after the media discovered and publicized the brief membership of Timothy McVeigh. If the militia members were concerned about protecting their part of the country from some kind of terrorism or tyranny, neither concern was mentioned during the afternoon that I spent with the group.

At some point the group did hold a business meeting of sorts in which several new members were introduced and a new system was described for contacting all the members in case of a natural disaster occurred. The leadership was particularly concerned about spreading the word in case of a forest fire, a tornado or the wreck of a train carrying poison chemicals or toxic gas.

I would estimate that maybe half of the 40 or so members who showed up brought along guns and spent some time at the range. Virtually every one of them had an AR-15 or other type of assault rifle, and they all had multiple, hi-cap mags. In the years since my visit with the Michigan Militia, an assault rifle seems to be almost a required item to be displayed by every militia member whenever such a group appears in a public space.

Here is the logo for the Michigan Wolverines, which is one of the militia groups which devolved out of the group I visited in 1991:

Militia groups which promoted an agenda more focused on resistance to liberal governmental structures and programs began to emerge with a greater degree of active and continuous behavior when Donald Trump began to pull away during the 2016 primary campaign with a narrative which spoke directly to some of the elements that combined to create the militia narrative which had been marginalized while Obama was at the head of the national helm.

But when Trump started to make references to the positive use of violence, such as his comments about getting votes even after he gunned someone down, the elements within the militia movement which saw themselves as preparing for physical and violent conflict with the liberal, national state, became even more committed to being a public presence which required them to be armed.

The presence of armed militia groups at public events, particularly events which promoted liberal, political organizations and/or programs, became a more frequent occurrence following the demonstrations held at Charlottesville, VA in August 2017. In this case, the militia was comprised largely of members of an American Nazi group who paraded down the street wearing Swastikas, chanting anti-Semitic slogans, and waving assault rifles in the air.

The presence of assault rifles is not, however, only evident when a militia group appears at a mass, public event. The demonstrators who marched around the Michigan State House to protest the Pandemic lockdown mandated by Governor Gretchen Whitmer in 2020 also were carrying assault-style guns. One of the GOP legislators, Beau LaFave, showed up at the Michigan State House with an AR-15 the night that the Governor delivered her 2020 State of the State address, but wasn't allowed to bring the gun into the legislative chamber. Two days later, the gun was stolen out of LaFave's house.

The public brandishing of assault rifles has made it difficult for the gun industry to continue promoting the idea that all guns which are available for public sale following a quick background check are 'sporting' guns and thus should not be considered weapons that serve any military or tactical use, even if they are being carried around by individuals dressed in tactical clothing and toting tactical or military gear. After all, as long as someone's clothing style is not illegal because it might be offensive to others, choosing how to dress while walking down the street with an AR-15 is just another manifestation of the Constitutional freedom which allows these individuals to own and openly carry a gun.

The issue of 'sporting' versus 'tactical' guns first emerged as a public narrative concern when the federal government began considering a ban on assault rifles in 1989, following a massacre of five children and injuries to scores of other young students in a Stockton schoolyard on January 17th. The shooter used an AK-47 which was legally owned, he was unemployed, and the shooting may have been provoked by his anger at the idea that new immigrants from the South were taking all the jobs.

In any case, the law to ban or restrict assault rifles required that the term 'assault rifle' had to be defined, so as to make a distinction between rifles whose ownership would now be more regulated than the ownership of other types of guns. The assault weapons ban that California implemented directly following the Stockton shooting, listed many specific guns that could no longer be sold but it also defined certain design features – folding stock, hand grip, bayonet lug, etc., - which would carry over to the federal assault weapons ban passed in 1994.

Even though these cosmetic design features were typical of guns carried by our military troops into battle, there was one fundamental difference between those weapons and the assault weapons banned first by California in 1989 and then by the Federal Government five years after the California probation went into effect - the difference having to do with how many rounds the guns would discharge every time the trigger was pulled.

The rifle carried by our troops since the mid-1960's has had a design which allows for more than one round to be fired when the trigger releases the sear, in one position every cartridge in the magazine is discharged, in the other position a pull of the trigger results in a three-shot burst. Allowing the soldier to shift the sear from full-auto to three-shot auto is referred to as selective fire which the civilian version of the AR does not have.

Civilians can purchase a full-auto rifle, known as a gun on the National Firearms List (NFA) but it is a lengthy and expensive licensing process which can only be conducted at the shop of a federally licensed Class III dealer, as opposed to a dealer who holds the much more frequently issued Class 1 Federal Firearms License (FFL).

Purchasing a gun on the NFA list also requires multiple background checks, and in some states also requires that the purchaser already holds a federal or state-issued license to collect guns or to own full-auto guns.

For all those reasons, it is estimated that there are somewhere around 60,000 full-auto guns in civilian hands, whereas the ownership of semi-auto assault weapons now numbers in the millions of such guns.

The gun industry has always tried to promote semi-auto assault rifles as just a different style of a sporting gun which can be used for hunting, or target shooting, or any other type of shooting activity which is not connected to military or tactical use of guns. The problem with this argument, however, is that it collapses when a group of militia members march down a street brandishing their AR-15's, dressed in military-style clothing and chanting slogans about 'protecting' the populace from the 'tyranny' of the state.

A bigger problem for the gun business in trying to pass of the AR-15 as just another 'sporting' gun is that the selective-fire feature on today's battle rifle, also allows the sear to be set for semi-automatic ammunition release. The reason for a soldier to have the ability to shoot his rifle like a 'sporting' gun has to do with the circumstances and logistics of modern warfare, which often takes place in crowded urban settings outdoors or, for that matter, within a house or an enclosed space, and such environments are much better suited for guns that discharge on a semi-auto basis where the ammunition discharge can be better controlled.

Given the way the bolt operates in a semi-auto AR-15 when the gases released by the shell's discharge first pull to eject a fired shell then push to place a fresh round in the breech, the shooter doesn't sacrifice that much time setting his gun on semi-auto rather than an automatic burst. At Sandy Hook, the shooter discharged more than 90 rounds in less than 3 minutes, a period of time that also required him to load at least two fresh magazines into the gun.

If we define a mass shooting as any event where four or more persons are killed or wounded in the same location or at the same period of time, then such shootings happen every day and do not require even the use of a semi-automatic pistol, even though such guns are almost always used for these types of shootings because they happen now to be the most typical handgun design being sold.

But since this book focuses on what we are referring to as 'rampage' shooting events, where double-digit and often large, double-digit industries occur, the weapon of choice used for such shootings, going all the way back to the Stockton schoolyard assault in 1989, is the civilian (semi-auto) version of the assault rifle, primarily because the gun is designed to use a magazine which holds 20 to 30 rounds or more, whereas semi-automatic pistols (Glock, Sig, et. al.) become cumbersome and difficult to move from one aim-point to another unless the magazine fits completely inside the butt of the run. Which means that a shooter wanting to discharge as many rounds as possible in a brief period of time will need to unload an empty magazine and insert a full magazine twice as often with a semi-auto pistol as with a semi-auto assault rifle.

Mass shootings which kill and injure in the double digits are occasionally accomplished with a pistol, and I mention several of these events in Chapter 1 (page 20). But in the 2007 shooting at Virginia Tech, where the largest number were killed and wounded until the 2016 shooting at the Pulse nightclub in Orlando, the shooter used a Glock but first barricaded himself inside and building which first responders couldn't enter until more than 40 minutes after the first shots were fired.

Until Donald Trump came along, and particularly in the years directly Timothy McVeigh blew up the Murrah Federal Building in Oklahoma City in 1995, armed militia groups kept to themselves and rarely, if ever participated in public, mass political events. This changed after 2016, and the fact that Trump couldn't find himself able to disown such organizations strongly and sharply after Charlottesville gave the militia a degree of normalcy that they hadn't enjoyed up until that time.

If anything, armed militia groups enjoyed something of a new lease on life when they began appearing in demonstrations against Covid-19 lockdowns which were often approved and bolstered by comments from Trump. The pendulum began swinging in the other direction and swinging very hard and fast after January 6th, 2021.

Whether groups like the Proud Boys and the Oath Keepers should be considered as being just larger and more politically conscious versions of militia groups who do not, as a rule, appear in an organized fashion at mass, public events, there is certainly a degree of shared behavior and outlook between many of the militias and groups like the Proud Boys who are characterized as militia groups by the digital media and the press.

There is one fundamental difference however, between these two types of militias, which is the groups which became prominent over the last several years as they demonstrated against Pandemic lockdowns and other liberal, political programs justify their existence only in terms of specific political ends, i.e., defending what they are attacks against the Constitution by the Deep State.

Smaller, geographically organized militia groups, of which there are several hundred at least, although many of these militias are paper or website organizations that have next to nobody actively enrolled, focus their activities on quasi-military preparedness to respond to any kind of mass threat, be it an invasion by hostile military forces or a collapse of the electric grid, or any other widespread disturbance which requires an organized response beyond what the government is prepared to do.

Most of the local militia groups profess a degree of conservative political beliefs because most Americans who own guns, particularly guns designed for self-defense, also happen to be situated on the right side of the ideological scale. On the other hand, the fact that people who support conservative politics join militia groups doesn't mean they are willing to engage in the kind of armed, violent behavior which broke out in front of and inside the Capitol on January 6th.

Yet the description of the January 6th rioters as having come to the District of Columbia armed and having used those weapons to breach the Capitol building and threaten or attack police and other security forces both outside and inside the Capitol, happens to ignore the degree to which these 'insurrectionists' showed up and engaged the forces of law and order without using guns. In fact, it was the police guarding the Senate chamber with drawn handguns who were armed with guns. I do not believe that a single individual who was arrested inside the Capitol and charged with disorderly conduct or worse was charged with possession of a gun.

There have been some outbreaks of violence within the context of militia groups, perhaps the most obvious example was the arrest of members of a militia group who were planning to kidnap Governor Gretchen Whitmer in 2020, a plot that was caught and prevented because the group was infiltrated by several FBI informants who pretended to be members of the militia group.

In fact, the linkage between militia membership and mass shootings is minimal at best, and even though militia narratives often focus on how the United States is threatened by the presence of various non-White, non-Christian groups, the rhetoric, and public display of assault weapons by militia groups has been much more a function of style rather than substance with little, if any gun violence being connected to these militia groups.

If anything, mass shooters tend to be loners and rarely, if ever, get involved with social groups or engage in group social activities in an ongoing way The ownership of an assault rifle may be typical of individuals who commit mass shootings, but there is no evidence which ties any general propensity to commit mass shootings to ownership of assault-style guns other than the degree to which the design and function of such guns make it easier to injure or kill multiple victims in one place or at one time.

5. ARE MASS SHOOTERS CRAZY?

Most mass shootings usually end with the death of the shooter, either a self-imposed injury or an injury committed by the response of police. On rare occasions a mass shooter is also stopped by another civilian who has access to a gun. But no matter which way a mass shooting event comes to an end, rarely do we get a post-event analysis of the shooter's thoughts or emotions before the slaughter takes place.

It is not that uncommon for mass shooters to be treated for behavioral/psychological issues before they plan and then put a big shooting into effect. Nancy Lanza, the mother of the Sandy Hook shooter, was killed by her son Adam before he got into his car and drove off to the grammar school. But she had put him into numerous mental health programs over the years, which evidently didn't work.

For that matter, the Virginia Tech student, Seung Hui-Cho, who set the record in 2007 for the number of victims he killed until the number was surpassed in the 2016 Pulse nightclub shooting in Orlando, had been treated for depression at a university health clinic and also briefly hospitalized in the four months prior to his mass assault, a period when he also was buying several guns.

We cannot find a single example of any individual who behaved in such an obviously mentally unfit fashion that someone was disposed to but did not contact the police, or someone actually contacted a public agency which then sent out a team to assess the degree to which the complaint was justified, and the subject was prevented from later carrying out a rampage act.

Dylann Roof, the 21-year-old who stormed into the Emanuel African-Methodist Episcopal Church in Charleston, SC and killed 9 people on June 17 2015, had expressed belligerent racist feelings towards friends but had never disclosed his plan to invade a Black church and attempt to murder everyone in the room during a Bible study class. The parents of the young man who drove 200 miles from his home to shoot 10 victims in a Buffalo supermarket had no idea that that their son harbored the racialist sentiments which evidently motivated his attack.

Even moments before mass killers begin their rampages, there are often few hints at what is about to take place. So, on the early evening of May 23, 2014, when a Santa Barbara City College student, Elliott Rodger, was stopped outside his apartment by police who had been sent to check his behavior at the request of his mother, they did not notice anything unusual about the way he answered questions covering his mental state. The police also neglected to ask Rodger whether or not he owned a gun.

Rodger went back to his apartment following his brief conversation with the cops, and later that evening stabbed his three roommates to death. He then exited the apartment, drove over to a campus sorority house, and tried to entrance but the door was locked. He then shot and killed two women outside the house, wounding a third.

By this time police had been notified and began chasing Rodger through the town, exchanging gunfire with him twice. During this drive-by he shot and killed a male student inside a deli, injured several pedestrians by ramming them with his car. His car then slammed into a parked car and went no further because Roger shot himself in the head.

The toll was 7 deaths and 14 injuries, a killing spree which Roger explained in a video uploaded to YouTube after stabbing his three roommates to death as each one walked into the apartment they shared. In the video, Roger claimed that he was going on a rampage because of the anger he felt by being rejected by multiple female students on the college campus, even though a majority of his victims were men.

What appears to be commonplace with virtually all the perpetrators of these gun rampages is that they plan these events well ahead of when the shooting actually begins to occur. The planning includes scouting out various locations both on terms of access and egress, whether the location is guarded or patrolled, how many potential targets are near or directly within the physical site, and of course building a private arsenal to accomplish the deed.

Finally, and most important, many mass shooters have been treated for mental distress or were being treated at the time of a mass shooting, but if there is a single individual who has ever confessed to a desire to slaughter large numbers of human beings which allowed for a professional intervention that eliminated the possibility of an attack, such behavior has yet to appear in any public discussion about such events.

If anything, what appears to be the more frequent backdrop to these events is the desire of the shooter to come out from relative anonymity and achieve notoriety based on what he has done. Or better yet, what he claims to have accomplished, because many rampage shooters believe and publicly announce that killing large numbers of people is part of a master plan which embodies important means to accomplish very important ends. This explanation was stated most explicitly by the greatest and most publicity-conscious mass shooter, Anders Breivik, who murdered 77 people at a park outside of Oslo in 2011 and made a point of allowing himself to be captured and sentenced to prison where he continues to promote himself to this very day.

After Breivik was arrested, but before he went to trial, he was examined by a psychiatric team to determine whether he would be charged with homicide or would be adjudicated mentally ill and therefore excused from facing a capital charge. The examination, which included lengthy interviews with Breivik, along with testimonies from family, co-workers, and friends, found him to be mentally ill.

Under Norwegian law, the psychiatric finding meant that he would be allowed to leave detention and rejoin society in a normal way if at some point hi mental illness either disappeared or was brought under control. For obvious reasons, this conclusion by the psychiatric team created an uproar in Norwegian society and forced the Court hearing the issue to require a second psychiatric examination conducted by a different group of psychiatrists to take place.

A year after the massacre, a second report on Breivik's mental status was delivered to the District Court and this report found Breivik to be sane and therefore mentally competent to stand trial for multiple counts of murder, which resulted in a 21-year sentence, which is the maximum punishment in Norway for a capital offense.

Breivik has returned to court multiple times since his initial incarceration. His petition to be paroled after ten years (which is allowed under Norwegian law) was denied, as were two lawsuits in which Breivik claimed that the conditions of his incarceration violated his human rights.

At the same time that Breivik has been challenging the conditions under which he is being confined, he also continues to promote his 1,500-page manifesto, *2083: A European Declaration of Independence,* which he emailed to more than 1,000 addresses the day before he exploded a bomb in downtown Oslo and then went out to Utoya to begin his murderous rampage.

In this document, Breivik developed a lengthy and convoluted history of the conflicts between Christianity and Islam, along with a critical appraisal of how European governments under the sway of liberal labor unions, were intent on destroying Western culture by encouraging immigration of Muslim populations into Norway and other Western countries. Basically, his views run parallel to what has become a movement known as 'Christian nationalism' which crops up on the far-right political fringe throughout the West.

Breivik is not the only mass shooter to create a public record of his intentions to commit carnage in a public space. Before killing his three roommates and then driving around Santa Isla shooting at random victims in the city's streets, Elliot Rodger uploaded a video to YouTube in which he explained his frustrations over being rejected by multiple women and predicted that there would shortly be a 'retribution' for everything he had suffered. The Sandy Hook shooter, Adam Lanza, did not create any documentary evidence about his plans to commit mass murders, but he evidently spent time on the internet researching stories about other individuals who committed wholesale violence using guns.

If there is one behavioral profile that distinguishes the individuals who commit these fearsome, mass shootings, as opposed to the perpetrators of gun violence who attempt to kill either a single individual or a few people gathered together in a small group (family gatherings, for example), it is the degree to which these mass shooting rampages are invariably planned well in advance of when they actually take place. The shooter often acquires the weapon and the ammunition months before the assault begins, he carefully investigates multiple shooting sites, he often does internet research about other mass shooting events, and rarely, if ever does he have any direct or personal connection to the victims of his assaults.

The characteristics of face-to-face shootings, even if they involve multiple victims and are therefore classified as 'mass' shooting events, are entirely different in virtually every respect. The shooter and the victim are almost known to one another, in domestic shootings they are related by marriage or blood. The shooter has a reason for wanting to shoot a specific individual, the location and time are of secondary or no importance at all. Most of all, individual shootings are spontaneous – hey occur because two or more persons get into an argument or despite of some kind, one of them or both have guns, out come the guns and someone is injured or dead.

Finally, and perhaps this is the biggest difference between the shooting rampages committed by Breivik, Holmes and others versus the daily, one-on-one shootings which occur randomly throughout the United States as frequently as one hundred times a day, is that the latter almost always occur within the immediate neighborhood of either the assailant or the victim, or both. What we might call in contrast to the mass shootings, the random, daily shootings, happen in certain neighborhoods all the time. These events are part and parcel, if you will, of everyday life. On the other hand, even when two big rampages occur within a ten-day span, such as what happened in Buffalo, NY, and Uvalde TX where 31 were killed and 20 injured on May 14 and May 24, 2022, such events are still infrequent when compared to daily gun assaults which may kill or injure three or four or even more.

We assume that individuals who commit random acts of gun violence against someone other than themselves are not 'crazy' or mentally disturbed. They are simply acting out aggressive behavior against someone they either don't like or someone who otherwise they believe might attack them. The fact that they use a gun means that they at least believe that having the weapon will give them some kind of advantage over an adversary, plus they know that a gun can create a much more definitive injury than would be accomplished any other way.

In other words, the kid who walks down the street with a gun in his pocket because he is expecting some kind of trouble or problem which can be more easily handled if he has access to a gun, isn't someone who doesn't know the difference between right and wrong. He just assumes that he'd rather be in trouble if he's caught with the gun than if he has to confront a threat and is unarmed.

On the other hand, when someone opens fire on a crowd and his only intention is to kill as many people as possible because he may or may not have some grievance which is somehow connected to that group, we assume that such an individual is somehow disconnected with the average person's understanding of 'right' versus 'wrong,' or at least lacks the ability to consider the consequences of what he has done.

We usually refer to such individuals as psychopaths, which is a term we apply to people who demonstrate anti-social behavior on a continuous basis, although such behavior can take many different forms and can be directed at a single individual rather than at a group.

The problem with trying to understand the behavior mechanisms which provoke the big, mass shootings is that most of the shooters do not outlive the shooting events, either because they shoot themselves or are shot by someone who intervenes with a weapon to shut down the event. If they are captured and come to trial for their crimes, such individuals rarely, if ever defend themselves based on being mentally disturbed and therefore not found criminally guilty for the damage they have done.

What should be understood about the shootings which result in more than four dead or injured victims is that such events exact a significant and unhealthy toll not just on the families and friends of the victims themselves, but of the entire community where the shooting rampage has occurred.

The town of Newtown, CT had to demolish the Sandy Hook Elementary School because too many residents of the town reported significant mental trauma every time they drove past the building after the shooting took place. The town of Uvalde, TX is likewise going to demolish the school building where 21 adults and children were gunned down.

Many neighborhoods and communities throughout the United States suffer more gun casualties every year than the number of individuals killed and wounded in any of the shooting rampages which take place. But this random violence is somehow considered if not 'normal' than at least expected to occur in communities like Chicago's West Side or North St. Louis or Brooklyn's East New York.

This type of internecine violence has not only been happening with a remarkable degree of frequency and continuousness over the past forty years, if not longer, but it rarely, if ever receives any public attention beyond a brief Monday media story since urban shootings tend more often than not to be weekend events.

Is there a connection between the daily, street carnage which claims between 40 and 50 Americans every day and the rare but much more dreadful mass killings which crop up every now and then? I deal with that question in the next and last chapter of this book.

6. THE DIGITAL DIVIDE.

In earlier chapters I discuss how changing manufacturing technologies made it easier and cheaper for the gun industry to make and promote the types of guns that are used in mass shootings. But to complete the story, we also have to consider how changes in the technology of making, selling, and buying guns has also led to a shift in product development towards the types of guns that turn up in most mass shootings, particularly the various models that follow from the basic AR-15.

One of the major changes in the whole retail landscape after World War II was the appearance of large, retail chain stores and the consequent disappearance of small, privately-owned local stores. This shift occurred primarily because the interstate highway system allowed manufacturers to ship large amounts of goods by truck, rather than by rail, which meant that rather than a city or town relying on distribution from a railroad depot, that goods could be moved from the point of manufacture directly to the retail store.

Not only did goods move with vehicular traffic, but so did the consumers who would buy these goods. I found myself in an enormous traffic jam at the intersection of two interstate highways which was located more than 40 miles from any town in either direction from where I sat hardly moving in my car.

The day was December 24, the last shopping day before Christmas, the intersection was in Oklahoma where Interstate 40 crossed Interstate 44, which is 60 miles west of downtown Oklahoma City. I thought the traffic jam was because of an accident. In fact, the backup was caused because the parking lot around a huge shopping center was completely filled and the exit ramps from both highways were also jammed with cars.

This incident occurred as I was driving across the country in 1975. It would be a common experience for any Last-minute Christmas shoppers over the next ten years. Why didn't some of these shoppers decide to buy their presents at a local store in town the following year? Because there was no local store in town unless they wanted to put a gun under the tree.

Until the last decade or so, the gun business was the only consumer-product business which still retained the two-step distribution model which was typical of all consumer-product retailing from when consumer products started to be purchased over the counter rather than from a catalog published by Sears. It was the advent of large, retail chains like Korvette's, Woolco and Ames (all founded in the 1950's, all defunct before 2000) which sounded the death-knell for the small, home-grown merchant on Main Street unless the store owner expanded his operation and rented space in the mall.

The retail gun business remained largely immune to these retailing changes for several reasons, not the least of which was that it was the point-of-sale that was regulated by the national gun laws of 1934, 1938 and 1968. These three laws required that anyone who wanted to sell guns as legal commerce needed first to be licensed in order to prove that he was law-abiding and therefore could have access to guns. The 1968 law also required that every licensed gun dealer keep careful records on the acquisition and disposition of all the guns which were bought and sold in the shop, records which could be examined at any time by Federal agents employed by the ATF.

The licensing and other regulatory issues connected to selling guns creates all kinds of management problems for chain stores, but the

bigger problem is that guns represent a potential public relations
headache for any chain-store operator, particularly if a chain outlet
becomes identified as the site where a gun was sold that was later used
in a crime, particularly a crime in which multiple victims were injured
or died. Given the fact that the retail margin on guns is about half the
margin on mass consumer items like clothing or hand tools, why risk
all the problems that a gun department could create when you can
stock that area inside the store with clothing or shoes?

In addition to the licensing and public relations difficulties which
kept the gun business in two-step distribution when every other
consumer product type shifted into chain stores, the thin retail
margins for guns tended to attract older, often retired men who could
supplement a small retail income with pension payments but were
long-time hobbyists who enjoyed playing around with guns.

Walk into the average gun shop in small town and the owner is
usually behind the counter deeply engaged in discussion or debate with
several other old gun-nut friends. The gun shop is often a community
clubhouse whose membership is usually a group of older, White men
who have been socially connected to one another through various gun
activities like gun shows and the sportsman's club.

For many of the older gun owners, buying and selling guns is as
much a part of their social identity as any other activity. In addition to
hanging out at the local gun shop, these folks never miss a gun show,
even if they have to drive 50 miles or more to get to where the show is
being held. They are also members of local shooting ranges or
sportsmen's clubs, which are also primarily venues for socializing with
gun-owning friends.

As active as these folks are in terms of socializing in and around
locations where there are lots of guns, they also don't represent

growth in the size of the gun market because basically they buy, sell and trade guns that are already owned and were initially sent by a gun factory to a wholesale house years ago. The gun industry has been trying endlessly to expand its market base to compensate for the deficit which has impacted the industry since hunting began to lose its appeal. In 1975, American hunters purchased 14 million hunting licenses. The same number of hunting licenses were purchased in 2020 but meanwhile, the country's population has doubled between those two dates.

What has changed in the gun world over the last two decades, however, is the degree to which guns are no longer bought over a retail gun shop's counter, but are purchased on the internet, a type of commerce that particularly involves guns used in mass shooting events.

Selling guns on the internet first started to gain attention when a website, *Gunbroker.com*, went online in 1999. The site allows private gun owners to list guns for sale and either choose to sell to the highest bidder in an auction format or sell the gun to a buyer who pays a fixed price. The website handles the financial transaction, but the seller then sends the gun to a dealer in the buyer's town, who conducts the background check and then transfers the gun for a fee.

*Gunbrok*er is one of a number of websites which allow buyers and sellers of guns and gun accessories to exchange money for products even if they live in different states and never have a face-to-face meet. The 1968 federal gun law ended all interstate gun shipments between individuals, so such transactions always involve a licensed dealer who both receives and then transfers the gun.

Since the background check form (Form 4473) does not contain any information about the origin of any particular gun which is going to be given to an individual after the background check is approved, there is no way of determining how many guns are bought and sold each month that come from a dealer's inventory as opposed to guns which were bought and sold between two private individuals who are required to make the transfer occur after a background check has been conducted at a gun shop.

In 2021, the Bloomberg gun-control group, Everytown, published the results of a study of online gun sales which focused primarily on advertisements for private sales on various websites where the seller lived in a state that did not require any kind of background check prior to selling the gun to someone else who lived in the same state. The study found that there were more than one million such advertisements on the websites that were reviewed, but the research group had no way of knowing either how many of these guns were ever sold or whether they ended up in the hands of someone living in a different state.

Since virtually all the guns listed for internet sales by private individuals (as opposed to internet gun ads placed by dealers, of which there are many such ads) are used guns, the internet has a built-in advantage for such commerce because the seller can list pictures of the gun to justify the selling price which is often a function of the condition of a used gun. Does the gun have an unblemished finish? Does a gun have all original exterior parts? The answers to such questions can make a considerable difference in the value of a used gun.

Such concerns have completely disappeared when we look at the online commerce involving the types of guns used in mass shootings, particularly the worst, most deadly events like Uvalde, Las Vegas, or Sandy Hook. The shooters in these locations used high-capacity assault rifles, all of which are manufactured with polymer frames, stocks and handles which require no maintenance at all. Polymer doesn't fade, it doesn't rust when subjected to high levels of humidity, it doesn't pick up blemishes from being dropped on the ground. And these factors add up to a gun that can be purchased online without even being seen by the individual who is forking over hundreds of dollars to buy a gun.

There is one other issue which has recently come into focus as regards the internet commerce in guns, and that is the degree to which gun makers and dealers are now using buy now, pay later plans to help move guns. The leading proponent in this regard is a finance company, Credova, which has gained notoriety because it provides financing for purchases of assault rifles manufactured by Daniel Defense, a gun maker who sells guns directly to consumers (although their guns are shipped to dealers to comply with the background-check law) and sold the guns that were used in three 2022 mass shootings in Uvalde, TX, Buffalo, NY and Highland Park, IL.

The use of online financing to sell guns is seen as making it easier for younger consumers to buy more expensive weapons, like an AR-15, and it may or may not be a coincidence that the three shooters at Uvalde, Buffalo and Highland Park were all under 21-years old when they purchased their guns.

There is no question that what drives the multi-billion market in video games are games where the contestants use automatic weapons to compete against one another even though such guns are rarely, if ever used in the commission of gun crimes. What these video games promote, however, is the normalcy of violence associated with guns. There has never been a serious study that has been able to establish a direct correlation between video shooting games and gun violence, but the idea of making violence *per se* a normal experience within the culture of young men is certainly a focus of video games.

At the same time, we do have studies which support the idea that movies created for the adolescent audience are increasingly violent at the same time that other threats to health, such as smoking, are now excised from mass culture as a deliberate attempt to create awareness of the kinds of dangerous behavior that young people should learn to avoid.

But the idea that guns do not represent a threat to health, particularly the kinds of rapid-fire guns that we see depicted in gun-action movies like the *John Wick* series, must have some influence on how certain individuals conceive plans to commit mass murders in a specific place and at a specific time.

Again, what always needs to be kept in mind when we try to figure out the mentality of individuals who commit mass shooting events, is that they may not have what we would consider a logical or reasonable motive for doing what they do, but they always go about doing it in a logical and reasonable way.

7. CONCLUSION.

The real problem in talking about behavior that results in the killing and wounding of scores of human beings in one place and at one time is not what we know about these shooters, but what we don't know. And because we don't know enough about the motives and feelings which drive someone on rare occasion to commit such a horrendous and fearsome act, we really have no basis for determining what sort of behavior might alert us to the possibility that someone we know is planning such an act.

Because the one thing we do know about the shootings which leave scores of individuals wounded and dead, is that they never occur in the quick, spontaneous, and unplanned way that most shootings take place. When it comes to how guns are used in the deaths and injuries suffered by the more than 275 Americans every day, to quote Lester Adelson, "With its peculiar lethality, a gun converts a spat into a slaying and a quarrel into a killing."

This description of gun violence is also typical of shootings where more than one victim is killed or wounded, which is why the idea of setting a numeric of 4 victims as defining a mass shooting really makes little sense. If we are going to adopt strategies to eliminate or at least reduce the daily toll America suffers from all types of gun violence, then at least we need to be careful and precise in how we think about the behavior which results in someone getting shot.

At the same time, we also need to focus attention on the industry whose products are used in mass shootings, and whether the advertising and messaging which promotes the sale of such products can also influence the behavior of the young men who increasingly show up as the individuals who commit these fearsome assaults.

When Charles Whitman climbed up to the top of the tower on the University of Texas campus and killed 18 persons and wounded another 31 in 1966, he used a bolt-action hunting rifle because he was barricaded inside a high-level perch and did not need mobility in order to find or scope his victims. In this respect, however, Whitman's shooting strategy, however, was quite unlike what has usually been employed by most mass shooters. With the exception of Steven Paddock, the 2017 Las Vegas shooter who blasted away from a hotel room far above where his targets were listening to a rock concert below, usually bring themselves quite close to the population which they are trying to injure or kill.

The victims at Sandy Hook were all within classrooms that Adam Lanza entered; the victims at the Pulse nightclub in Orlando were within a few feet of the assailant; the victims at the recent attacks in Uvalde, TX, and Buffalo, NY were also directly adjacent to the perpetrator in those events.

Along with arming themselves with guns that are similar, if not exact copies of weapons used by military troops, it is not unusual for perpetrators of mass shootings to dress themselves up in tactical gear which makes it appear that they are engaging in some kind of military assault. Increasingly such equipment is carried in retail gun shops and also shows up in displays at local gun shows and national trade shows. The NRA annual show, for example, has a whole floorspace area devoted to tactical equipment, including clothing, optics, and other military-style accessories such as tactical vests like the kind pictured here:

The company which manufactures this vest not only refers to it as a tactical accessory, but its advertising refers to this article as a piece of 'survival' equipment. Now why someone living in the United States would need to spend $40 (the retail cost of this vest) on this item in order to enhance his chances of surviving is left to the fantasies of the consumer. But mass shooters wearing such gear are not uncommon and in many instances these shooters end up exchanging gunfire with police and perhaps these vests are worn in anticipation of the event drawing return fire from law enforcement or armed civilians at the scene.

This shift towards a more militaristic focus for products produced by gun makers and accessory manufacturers was not the way in which the rifles used in most mass assaults were initially marketed to potential buyers. In fact, the gun industry initially went out of it sway to bring such products into the hands of consumers by describing them as 'sporting' products, a word which meant hunting or other outdoor use of guns, but never would be a term applied to anything having to do with military applications.

In 2008, I briefly considered importing a 22-caliber, target rifle with Olympic-grade accuracy but at a modest retail price. I first attempted to copyright the term 'modern sporting rifle' but the application was denied because the term had been used many times previously. I then purchased two internet URLs – *modernsportingrifle.com* and *modernsportingrifle.org*.

I brought several prototypes of the rifle to the national gun show, the SHIOT show, and displayed the guns in a small booth. Midway through the show I was approached by a counsel from the National Shooting Sports Foundation (NSSF) which sponsored the SHIT show. He asked if I would sell the two URLs to the NSSF, and we ended up making a deal in which they would own the URLs and I would get a better booth placement at the next year's show.

Why did the NSSF want to own these URLs? Because as the counsel explained to me, several of the major chain stores like Cabela's were concerned about selling military-style guns in their locations which were family-shopping destinations: "We aren't comfortable selling what appears to be military guns in a store where women and mothers will go shopping with their kids."

Shortly after I signed over those URLs to the NSSF, they added a page about modern sporting rifles to their website which reads as follows: "These rifles are used by hunters, competitors, millions of Americans seeking home-defense guns and many others who simply enjoy going to the range. Despite their popularity, modern sporting rifles are widely misunderstood. Why? Confusion exists because though these rifles look like military rifles, they do not function the same way."

Note the statement that the modern sporting rifle does not function like a military gun. This was true when the NSSF first added this page to their website and started to promote the sale of modern sporting rifles because at that time the military gun fired in full-auto mode whereas the civilian version of the assault rifle was a standard, semi-automatic gun.

This alleged differentiation between the military and civilian rifles is no longer true. The current battle rifle issued to U.S. troops can be set either to fire in 3-shot bursts or in semi-automatic mode, exactly the way the current AR-15 works. So, if a soldier sets the gun to fire semi-auto, is this trooper going into battle with a 'sporting' gun? Of course not. And the NSSF has not made any change in the website text to reflect this engineering similarity between the military and civilian guns.

Obviously, whatever concerns the gun industry held about selling a military look-alike product has long since disappeared. In fact, current assault-rifle marketing plays up the personal defense and military-tactical use of the guns. So, for example, the website for Daniel Defense, whose guns were used in mass shootings in Buffalo, NY and Uvalde, TX, promotes their guns as being applicable to sport shooting, personal defense, and professional arms, with the professional shooter looking like this:

When Colt Firearms purchased the original M-16 design from Gene Stoner and began manufacturing the gun for military use in 1964, the company also issued a civilian, semi-automatic model, the original AR-15, which they referred to as the Colt 'sporter' that same year. Here's how that gun is now advertised on the Colt website:

In other words, the gun industry has completely overcome any fear of the assault rifle as being considered a military weapon. In fact, to the extent that the gun is now touted as what should be used for 'home defense,' the entire narrative has now shifted to embracing the idea that this weapon is designed to be used against human targets which, by definition, has no connection to any sporting use at all.

I am going to end this brief book with the following observation about mass shootings and the types of guns that are usually found in the hands of mass shooters. The only time that the United States was ever invaded or threatened by invasion by the military of another county was when Robert E. Lee brought the Army of Northern Virginia into Maryland in 1863. Otherwise, every single armed conflict between the United States and some other country has occurred somewhere outside our national borders.

The United States has also never lost a war, if we mean by using the word 'lost' a delegation representing our country showing up at some peace treaty and signing a legal document which declared another government to be 'victors' in a conflict against us. Granted, we got chased out of Viet Nam in 1973 and pulled out of Afghanistan in 2021. But if anything, over the nearly thirty years between those two events, the country has become much more invested in a military-style culture with the 'peace movement of the 1960's and 1970's a vague memory if it is recalled at all.

Much of this contemporary militarism, of course, is a function of the War on Terror and the degree to which we now use the word 'terrorism' to describe not just violence perpetrated by national enemies, but mass shooting and other violent behavior committed by American citizens as well.

Not only have we become immured to the existence of terrorist acts within our own country, the United States is also a society which seems to hold a built-in belief in the dangerousness of our society, even though both terrorist attacks by American-born or foreign-born Muslims are rare events and the national per-100K homicide rate today is half of what it was in the early 1980's.

Given the degree to which our society holds views on threats of violence which are not aligned with reality, or the degree to which the average person might be a victim of a violent event, should we be at all surprised that younger men want to go out and purchase a military weapon for which there is no objective need of ownership at all?

When I was ten years old, I saved up enough money to go down to the corner hardware store and buy myself a Daisy Red Ryder b-b gun. I spent hours in my back yard playing with that gun, usually pretending that I was a trooper with the U.S. Cavalry engaged in a fight to the death with Cochise and some Indian band.

It never once occurred to me to use that weapon or *any* weapon to transform my little, backyard fantasies into a real-life event. But when I was a teenager, I played basketball with a kid my age down the block who walked into a college library when he was twenty years old and stabbed his ex-girlfriend to death. If he had been able to purchase an assault rifle, maybe he would have walked into that library and kill everyone in the room.

I can tell you that there was absolutely nothing in his behavior or the behavior of his parents and sister that could have made me or anyone predict that some day he would wake up with a loose screw in his head. But he did. And he did in the same way that mass shooters like the kid who shot up Sandy Hook or the kid who shot up Robb Elementary woke up one morning with loose screws in their heads.

I wish I could end this book by explaining such behavior, but I can't. And neither can anyone else.